UNUSUAL PANZERS

Horst Scheibert

Schiffer Military/Aviation History
Atglen, PA

Photo Credits:
Federal Archives-Photo Archives, Koblenz (BA)
Federal Archives-Military Archives, Freiburg (BA)
U.S. Army Photographs, Washington
Nowarra Archives
Podzun Archives

Translated from the German by Dr. Edward Force.

Printed in the United States of America.
ISBN: 0-88740-681-5

This book was originally published under the title,
Deutsche Spezialpanzer,
by Podzun-Pallas Verlag.

We are interested in hearing from authors with book ideas on related topics.

Published by Schiffer Publishing Ltd.
77 Lower Valley Road
Atglen, PA 19310
Please write for a free catalog.
This book may be purchased from the publisher.
Please include $2.95 postage.
Try your bookstore first.

Note:
In the German Wehrmacht there were many kinds of special tanks for a variety of tasks. But since they were either built only in small numbers (sometimes only prototypes) or were built only in the last years of the war, there are few photos of them in existence today. In this volume we portray tanks for engineering tasks and recovery tanks – to the extent that the latter have not been shown in earlier books.

I would like to express my thanks to my longtime friend Reiner Rössle, who prepared the majority of the drawings for this book. Since very few photographs exist of the vehicles examined, he played an important role in allowing me to present a well-rounded and inclusive picture of a little-known weapon, the German engineer tank. Thanks are also due to Prof. Dr. Wolfgang Sawodny for his generous support of this work.

Foreword
Along with the battle tanks and self-propelled guns, there gradually developed, based on need, tracked vehicles for a variety of tasks within the armored troop units, particularly for their engineer (Pionier) units. The development of such minesweepers and bridgelayers was begun quite early, but as the war went on and raw materials became scarce, they had to give priority to battle tanks, and thus were no longer developed beyond the protype stage, or never left the drawing board. The Western Allies, with their abundance of raw materials, were able to prove, through their use in large numbers, the effectiveness of such special tanks, which are accepted as necessary components of the armies.

Somewhat more extended development was devoted by Germany to the problem of an armored ammunition transporter, which did see service, though in small numbers, before the end of the war. Most extensive of all was the production and utilization of tracked, remote-controlled explosive-charge carriers, which were built in various sizes and versions, of which the so-called "Goliath" was the most widely known. Therefore the main portion of this book is devoted to them, while the book also, for the first time, includes related material on the engineer tanks and special vehicles. The recovery tanks have also been included, which were of particular need to the repair-shop units with the use of the heavy and expensive Tiger and Panther battle tanks, but which were also never available in sufficient numbers.

Explosive Charge Carriers

R.RÖSSLE '80

Introduction

As soon as World War II began, the problem of moving explosive charges toward obstacles and the like while under fire became apparent, and attempts were made to provide armored protection to the engineers for this purpose. A quickly produced temporary solution was the equipping of the Panzer I with a sliding ramp on the rear to carry a 75 kp explosive charge. To unload it, the tank was driven backward to the target, the anchorings of the charge were loosened, and the charge slid to the ground under its own weight, Delayed ignition made it possible for the vehicle to get away before the explosion. In 1940 this very primitive system was developed further by attaching a swinging arm, controlled from inside, to place the explosive charge. In the same year, the HWA got the idea of a remote-controlled charge layer and entrusted the Borgward firm with the design of a suitable unmanned miniature tank that would receive its commands through a cable. This development culminated with the two versions of the Goliath described in detail on page 10, one with an electric, the other with a gasoline motor. The vehicle had the explosive charge built into it and was thus destroyed by the explosion. At the same time, efforts were being made at Borgward to make the remote controls already installed in the B I (see page 32) usable for an armored charge carrier.

The first version of Charge Layer I, which unloaded the 75 kg explosive charge on a ramp attached to the rear end of the vehicle.

This rear view of the Charge Layer I, used in the west in 1940, shows clearly the two guiding rails of the ramp. The explosive charge is fastened to the upper end of the ramp. To unload it, the tank was driven backward to the target and the charge was let loose, whereupon it slid to the ground under its own weight. (BA)

Combined with the lengthened running gear of the Ammunition Carrier VK 301/302 (described on page 28), there resulted the heavy explosive charge carrier B IV (see page 5), first built in 1942, which unloaded its charge at the target via a steep grade, got away before the explosion, and thus had multiple uses. Both the Goliath and the B IV were built until shortly before the war ended, several thousand being produced in various versions. While the Goliath was usually used singly against immobile targets (bunkers, etc.), the B IV was used in groups to form special radio-controlled (FKL) tank companies, subordinated to a Panzer or Panzerjäger unit. They were utilized for combat reconnaissance, blowing alleys in minefields, removing targets that were hard to fight otherwise,

and attacking the heaviest enemy tanks. The Panzer unit that followed them was to provide covering fire for the remote-controlled tanks and secure the ground that they won. In 1944 attempts were made to overcome this double-track system when a successor model for both vehicles was planned, in which all the previously gained experience was to be combined. The "Springer" medium explosive charge carrier (see page 24) developed by NSU in Neckarsulm was radio-controlled like the B IV but could not unload its explosive charge and thus destroyed itself along with its explosive charge, like the goliath. By the end of the war, though, only fifty of these progressive vehicles could be built, of which no more than three reached the troops.

Below: In 1940 the firm of Talbot in Aachen was commissioned to build a new unloading mechanism for the Charge Layer I. The explosive charge was now attached to the end of a 2.75-meter swinging arm, which could be controlled from inside the vehicle. The great length of the holding apparatus also allowed the charge to be unloaded in front of the tank. Like the version of the Charge Layer I already described, only a few test models of this version were built.

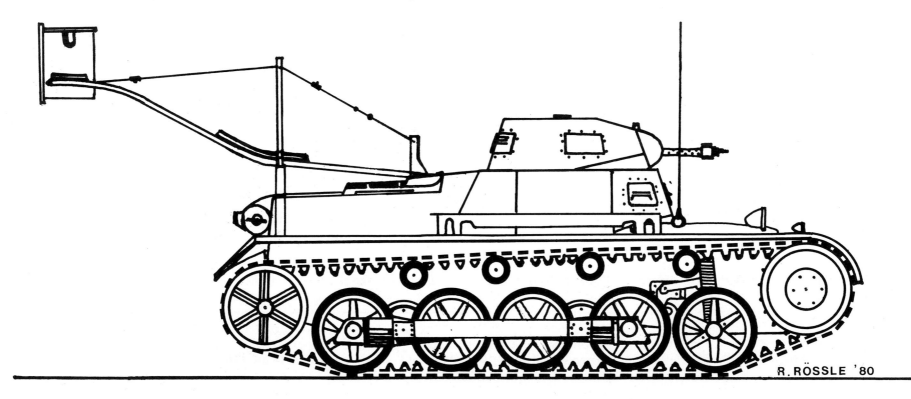

R. RÖSSLE '80

Heavy Explosive Charge Carrier B IV

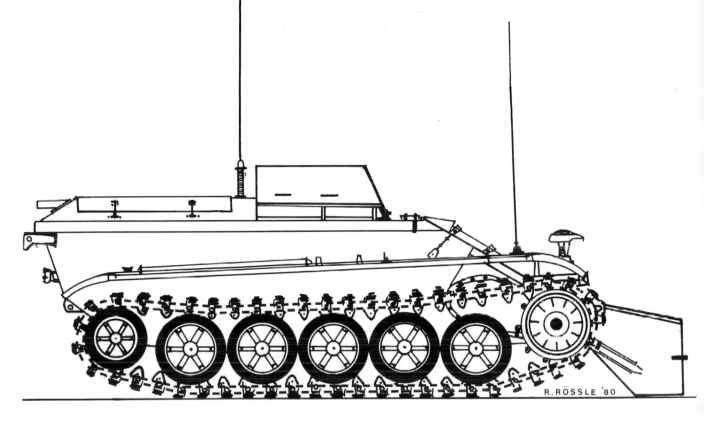

R. RÖSSLE '80

The Heavy Explosive Charge Carrier B IV was the result of further development of remote-controlled miniature mine-removing tanks of types B I and B II (see p. 32 for description), which had already been advocated for the special engineers by the High Command of the Army, but which had not performed especially well in tests. The Borgward firm, which had built these mine removers, therefore modified them in 1941 into the Explosive Charge Carrier B IV, after the Wehrmacht had reported a need for such vehicles. The remote controls of the B IV, produced by the firm of Hagenuk in Kiel, operated by radio and had a maximum range of two kilometers. The charge layer was, of course, brought to the scene of action by a driver, who sat in the middle of the vehicle. The driver's seat was protected from fire by 8 mm armor plates, which were usually folded to the side so that the driver could observe the battlefield better. The 49 HP engine, located in the rear, sent its power, via a shaft to the left of the driver, to the two front drive wheels and thus to the tracks. The 500 kg explosive charge was housed in a wedge-shaped container that was held on the nose of the vehicle by two swinging arms. This attachment could be released by means of exploding rivets, either mechanically or by radio. The container,

set in motion by its own weight, then slid down a 47-degree ramp. The delayed ignition of the charge allowed the vehicle to be moved out of the danger zone in time and thus saved from destruction. The Heavy Charge Carrier B IV went into series production in 1942 as Sd. Kfz. 301, Type A. The Type B, produced as of 1943, differed from its predecessor only in details, but was 0.4 ton heavier. At

the end of 1943, a considerably more powerful engine, producing 78 HP, was installed. Since the rear compartment had to be enlarged for it, the appearance of the vehicle also changed strikingly. In December 1944, the production of the B IV (Type C) was halted because of the war situation. In all, 1193 of Sd. Kfz. 301, including all the variations, had been delivered to the troops.

Left: As of April 1942, Borgward delivered the version of the B IV shown here to the troops. The assembly of the vehicle was done by Borgward, but the hull had to be produced and delivered by the Dortmund-Hoerder-Verein. The exhaust pipe at the rear, usually impossible to see, shows clearly in this picture.

Right: The chassis of the B IV had five road wheels, mounted close together on torsion bars. The power was transmitted from the motor to the two forward toothed wheels by a driveshaft, the Clectra steering gear attached to it, and finally the transmission. (BA)

Above: The B IV, hard to identify here, was to remove static obstacles from the path of the following tanks. After it had brought its payload to the target, it was brought back to its starting point by remote control before the charge exploded, and prepared for its next mission. (BA)

Upper right: This B IV, used in Crimea in 1942, is being overhauled by a mechanic. All the components of the power train were easily accessible through servicing hatches in the deck of the vehicle. (BA)

Right: Here, under the critical eyes of several officers, the remote-controlled laying of 500 kg explosive charges, held in wedge-shaped racks on the fronts of the vehicles, is being tested. By means of exploding rivets, the link between the charge and the vehicle could be broken; set in motion by its own weight, the charge then slid to the ground, as can be seen in this picture. Then the B IV was moved by radio control out of the danger zone of the explosive, which was fitted with a delayed ignition. (BA)

Left: This captured vehicle is missing its explosive charge, the front road wheel was torn from its swinging arm by the explosion, and the side armor, only 12 mm thick, was slightly damaged. (US Army photograph)

Right: In addition to the "Goliath" light explosive charge carrier, the Germans also used its big brother, the B IV, against the Allied forces that landed at Anzio. This B IV Type B was knocked out of action by a mine and is being inspected by specialists of the 1st British Infantry Division before being taken away. (US Army photograph)

These three pictures show a B IV Type C, built from the end of 1943 to December 1944, that was captured by the American forces. It had been modified from the original version. To hold the new six-cylinder engine that produced 78 HP, the rear end had to be extended upward noticeably and the length of the vehicle extended by 40 centimeters. This extension of the external dimensions, plus armor plate 4 mm heavier than that of types A and B, brought about a 1.4-ton increase in its fighting weight, to 5 tons. The picture at right shows clearly the damaged rack that held the 500-kg explosive charge. The covering plate is missing, the explosive material has been removed and probably disarmed.

Light Explosive Charge Carrier "Goliath"

In 1940 the Army Weapons Office contracted with the Borgward firm to develop a miniature tracked vehicle that would be capable of carrying a 50-kilogram explosive charge. After a development time of two years, the first test models were delivered in April 1942. The vehicles were powered by two electric motors built by the Bosch firm and taking power from two batteries. Unlike the B IV, remote control was done by means of a cable that was unrolled from a drum in the rear as the vehicle moved forward. The maximum range of this vehicle, listed officially as Sd. Kfz. 302, was only 1.5 km, limited by the meager performance of the electric powerplant. Therefore the Army Weapons Office decided to replace the electric motor with a gasoline engine. Since this modification took up a good deal of time, the Sd. Kfz. 302 with the electric motor remained in production until January 1944.

These two photos clearly show the external differences between the two versions of the "Goliath." At left is the first type built, with electric motor (E), and at right the gasoline-powered version (V Version) produced as of 1943. The V Version lacks the side battery boxes, having instead a modified engine cover with cooling louvers. The number of upper road wheels could also be reduced from the three of the electrically powered "Goliath" to two, spaced farther apart, which required a different track guiding. Thus the rear leading wheel was moved farther down and, instead of a complete disc wheel, became a spoked type. On the covering panel of the E Version, which was straight, a covered air exhaust for the motor cooling system and the fuel fillers were attached. The opening for the starter can also be seen behind the hood of the air intake. (2xBA)

In all, 2650 of them were delivered. The first light charge carriers with gasoline engines came off the assembly line in March 1943. There were scarcely any external changes; only the number of return rollers had been reduced from three to two. Another identifying mark of the V version, which was designated Sd. Kfz. 303, was the air intake attached to the roof, while the side battery cases were eliminated. A two-cylinder Zündapp motor provided 12.5 horsepower and extended the range to 12 kilometers. There were two minor variants of Sd. Kfz. 303, and a and a b type, which mainly varied only in the different weight of the explosive charge (75 and 100 kg). The charge was carried in the front of the hull. In all, 5079 of these vehicles reached the troops before the war ended.

They used the "Goliath" (as the charge carrier was also called) to remove obstacles and attack fixed enemy positions. When the charge was detonated, the vehicle was destroyed too and thus could not be reused as could the B IV. The Goliath was taken to where it would be used on a specially built two-wheel transporter.

Two engineers pull the "Goliath" (E) through the brush and into action on the two-wheel handcart made especially for it. (BA)

Here the two-man crew has released their "Goliath." Unlike the B IV, it was not controlled by radio, but directed by a wire that unrolled. (BA)

This picture gives an impression of the off-road capability of the "Goliath", seen here climbing a slope at full speed. (BA)

Well hidden behind the bushes, the crewmen wait for a chance to send their "Goliath" against the enemy. The opening in the cover of the battery and engine compartment, through which a bolt could be passed to attach the vehicle to its two-wheel handcart, can be seen here.

The five pictures on these two pages show the steps in "Goliath" action. First the charge carrier behind the HKL is unloaded from its two-wheel transport cart (above) and then moved to the foremost lines under its own power and checked. (left)

Above: Well camouflaged, the crew takes up positions at the edge of the forest and waits for the enemy.

Right: A Soviet SU 85 assault gun breaking through the lines will fall victim to the "Goliath." Because of its small size, it was hard for the enemy to put it out of action with a direct hit —despite its low speed of only 10 kph afforded by the two Bosch motors which together produced 13.6 HP.

Left: The "Goliath" was also used against the Allied forces landing at Anzio in Italy, though with little success. No fewer than 14 vehicles were destroyed by small-arms fire in one day before they could reach their targets. Another possibility was cutting the control cable, whereby the vehicle was stopped and could easily be disarmed. In this picture, an American sergeant is inspecting the interior of an immobile "Goliath." The drum for the control cable and the battery in its box to the side are easy to see (the cover is gone). (US Army photograph)

Above: This "Goliath" was also destroyed at the Anzio front without detonating its charge. Here too, the side cover plate was torn off, so that the battery (left) and one of the two electric Bosch motors (right) can be seen.

During the D-Day invasion on the coast of France, remote-controlled explosive charge carriers were used against the Allies. In the Utah Beach sector, though, not one of them reached its target. This picture was taken there and shows explosives experts of the US Marines disarming two immobile E-type "Goliaths" after a hard fight on the beach.

Probably halted by a defect, this well-camouflaged "Goliath" has stopped though its control cable is intact. It is being watched by American infantrymen in Normandy.

Opposite page: As of March 1943, the overworked gasoline-powered version of the "Goliath" was delivered. In place of the two electric motors, a Zündapp gasoline engine of approximately the same power was installed. The action radius of the "Goliath" was thus increased decidedly. With a full tank, which was located in the rear of the tank and held six liters, the explosive charge carrier now had a maximum range of 12 km. In this picture, the motor is just being started with a crank. The slit through which the control cable runs can also be seen; the structure behind it was meant to prevent getting off track. (BA)

The soldier in the picture above is holding the controls of the "Goliath." The steering impulses ran through the cable to two electromagnetic couplings that were engaged either simultaneously or individually by the man in control. Thus the vehicle was steered straight ahead, to the left or right. (BA)

Right: This "Goliath" was not brought to the scene of its action on a two-wheeled handcart, as usual, but on a truck. After unloading it, the crew examines the miniature tank. (BA)

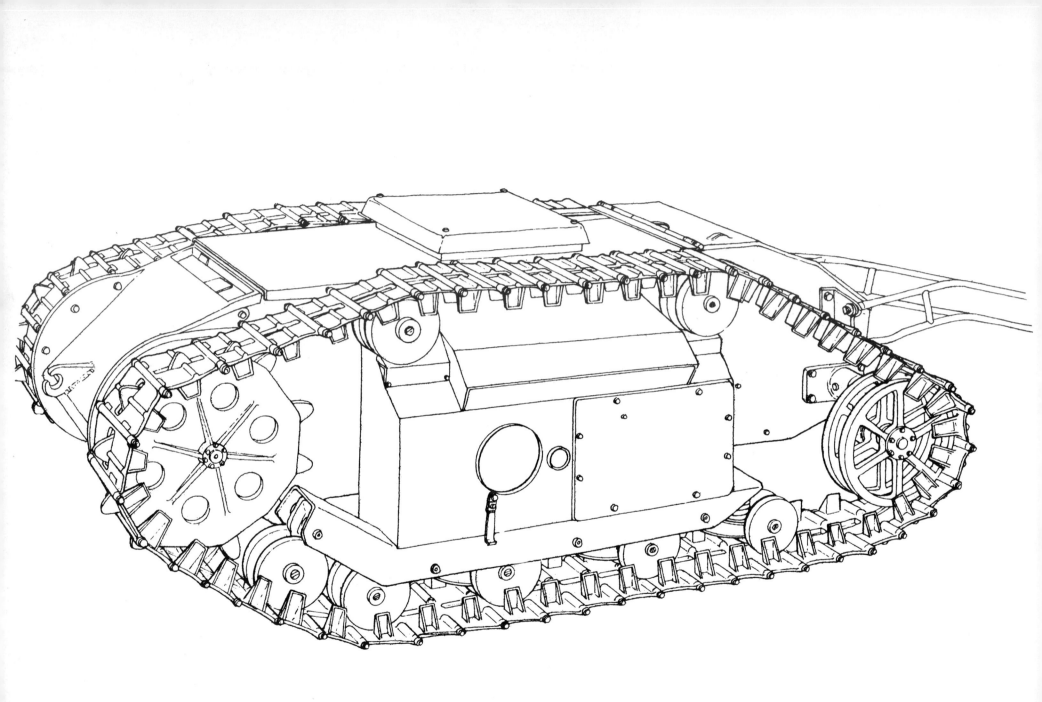

Above: In this bizarre rural landscape – presumably an army camp – the "Goliath" is being tested. (BA)

Right: These two pictures show the "Goliath" in action on the eastern front. The remote-controlled vehicle carries its load through a desolate garden at the edge of a village. (2xBA)

Left: When the Warsaw uprising was put down in August 1944, explosive tanks of the "Goliath" type were utilized. The two-wheeled transport carts could also be towed by trucks. Here they are just being uncoupled. Besides being fastened by the lateral attachments, the "Goliath" was also secured to the cart at the front in order to prevent the axle from bending. (BA)

Above: After being detached from the truck, the transport carts with their dangerous load are moved by manpower to their scenes of action in the contested city. (BA)

Right: This "Goliath" was completely destroyed and left beside a road in Italy during the 1944 retreat. In the background its transport cart, likewise badly damaged. By the end of the war, some 7700 "Goliaths" had been built, roughly 5050 with gasoline engines and 2650 with electric motors. (BA)

Left: Two gasoline "Goliaths", already loaded on transport carts, await action in a shed. The air scoop, which became necessary for the gasoline engine, is very easy to see on the vehicle in front.

These three electric "Goliaths" were captured by American forces on the French coast before they could be used by the Germans. (US Army photograph)

This photo affords a good view of the interior of the "Goliath" miniature tank. The front chamber held the 100-kilogram load of explosive, while the engine is in the rear chamber. The fan for the air filter can be seen at the center of the vehicle.

Medium Explosive Charge Carrier "Springer"

The "Springer" medium explosive charge carrier developed by NSU at Neckarsulm in 1944 was meant to replace the two vehicles of this type produced to then, the "Goliath" and B IV. As a result of the war situation, which became more and more serious, efforts were made at NSU to make the later production process as simple as possible. Therefore the design utilized the chassis, extended to five road wheels, of a tracked vehicle also produced in the NSU factory. To be sure, the prototypes of this kind that were built proved, when tested, to have insufficient off-road capability. The addition of another road wheel to the second design, it was believed, would improve this. The resulting version was, like the B IV, directed either by remote control or manually from a driver's seat at the rear, but the 350-kilogram explosive charge could not be removed, so that the "Springer" had to be destroyed when it was used. Unlike the later production vehicles, those of the so-called zero series had their tracks protected by 3 mm sheet metal attached to the sides. The original difficulties with the cooling of the 28 HP engine was eliminated by raising the engine cover somewhat. In October 1944, production and assembly of the first series of "Springers" began at NSU. The hulls needed for assembly were provided by the firms of Bohemia (Böhmisch-Leipa" and Jessen (Hamburg-Wandsbek). In all, fifty vehicles could be produced before the end of the war, but only three of them reached test units at the front.

Above: Since the off-road capability of the first "Springer" prototypes left something to be desired, the running gear had to be modified. A pre-production model of this new vehicle, which still had track aprons on the sides, which were later to be eliminated, is seen in this photo. Several of its characteristics, such as the exhaust pipe, the engine air intake and the covering of the driver's seat – here folded down – can be seen clearly. (BA)

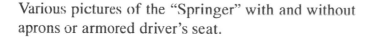

Various pictures of the "Springer" with and without aprons or armored driver's seat.

Above: A look at the NSU "Springer" production line, destroyed by bombs. All the vehicles are missing the front covering plate for the motor. The three protective panels over the driver's seat are folded up, as was done for marching. Note the very narrow track, the small surface of which was probably responsible for the vehicle's poor off-road performance. In the background, individual parts of the "Springer" are stored – road wheels, body panels, etc.

In the photo at the upper right, Generaloberst Guderian examines a late version of the "Springer and a B IV explosive charge carrier.

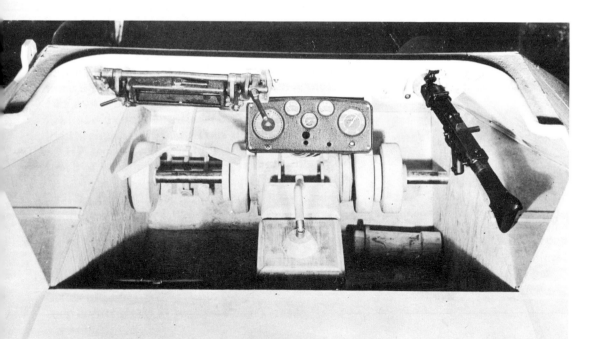

Upper left and above: The wooden mockup of the VK 501, development of which as assigned to the Weserhütte firm, after the already described VK 301 failed to live up to expectations in troop testing. In addition to a four-man crew, 500 kilograms of ammunition were to be carried in a cargo space of one cubic meter. For short-range defense, a machine gun was mounted at the nose, as can be seen in the wooden model. In addition to its original use as a supply vehicle, the VK 501 was also capable of being used for combat reconnaissance and transportation of wounded men. To be sure, limits were set by the top speed, which was reduced by half (30 instead of 60 kph, as it was intended to install a production truck engine producing 90 HP in the six-ton VK 501). (2xBA)

Left: A look inside the wooden mockup shows the driver's seat at left with the usual foot pedals used in tanks and the adjustable lookout slit; in the middle is the meager instrument panel. (BA)

Above: Since the development of independent fully tracked transport vehicles progressed only slowly, attempts were made to meet the demand for such vehicles temporarily by rebuilding the chassis of production tanks. This was a very early attempt, made by Krupp and Daimler and based on a Panzer IA. The hull of the turretless vehicle served as storage space, and the opening in the body for the turret was simply closed with opening armor plates. Thus the tank was turned into an ammunition carrier (Sd.Kfz. 111). (BA)

Upper right: This picture shows the chassis of a Panzer II and Panzer III (Type B, C or D) side by side, both turned into makeshift ammunition transporters. (BA)

Right: As the vehicle was never built, only this drawing remains of a plan to rebuild the Panzer IV into an ammunition carrier. The only supply vehicle on the Panzer IV chassis was the Ammunition Tank IV Type F, built especially to supply the 60 cm "Karl" mortar.

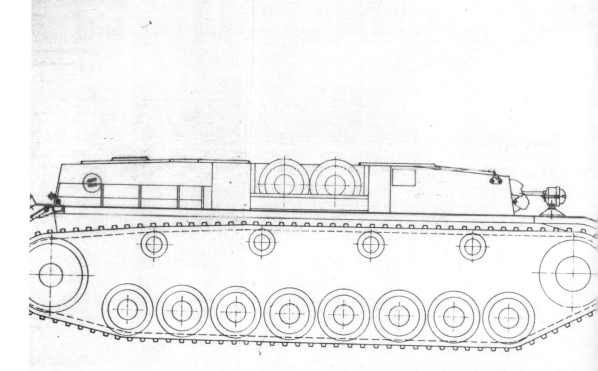

Minesweepers

At the very beginning of World War II, in 1939, the commander of the Army requested a small mine remover for the special engineers. The mines were to be made to explode by towed rollers. So that the vehicle would not be damaged, the body was to be cast completely in concrete. After a one-year development period, Borgward was able to present a test model of the minesweeper, designated B I, in January 1940. The prototypes of this early development already had not only the control elements intended for manual driving installed, but also a remote-control system built by the Hagenuk firm on Kiel, though the fifty production vehicles finished by May 1940 lacked the latter. While the B I type was being delivered by Borgward, another 100 units of a strengthened version of the mine-removal car were ordered. The new version was designated B II and differed from the first type only in its gross weight, which was increased from 0.8 to 2.4 tons, and the more powerful motor that resulted. Apparently, though, the method using removal rollers did not achieve much success in action, so that further production in the same year did not take place. The vehicle was then developed by Borgward into the B IV heavy explosive charge carrier described on page 5. The Krupp firm in Essen had been working on the design of a bigger, heavier mine-removal vehicle since 1940. At the end of the project studies carried out by Krupp, a prototype of the 130-ton vehicle called "Räumer S" was built in 1944. Unlike

the previous developments, this was designed as a wheeled vehicle and consisted of two equal halves linked together by a driveshaft and hydraulic cylinder. In addition to these two special vehicles, Panzer III and IV tanks were also modified into minesweepers. Like the other developments, they got no further than the experimental stage. Thus the German Wehrmacht had no armored minesweepers in action in large numbers – unlike the western Allies, who developed an incredible lot of ideas in this realm and had an extensive arsenal of such vehicles, particularly those based on the Sherman and Churchill tanks.

One of the fifty B I mine removal vehicles, designated Sd. Kfz. 300 (Type I). The body, cast in concrete and intended to protect the vehicle from damage by the mines detonated by the towed rollers, can be seen well. Along with this version, there was also one that weighed only 0.8 tons and differed externally only in having one more road wheel in its running gear (B II). (BA)

Below: The Panzer IV was also fitted experimentally with mine rollers. Unlike the German Wehrmacht, which had to do without series production of such accessories on account of the unfolding course of the war and the advancing shortages of raw materials, many standard British and American tanks of the Sherman, Churchill and other series were equipped with similar devices and made good use of them, particularly in the 1944 invasion and the battles that followed. (BA)

Above: When the war ended, the only finished prototype of the "Räumer S" was captured by American troops. This picture gives an idea of the vehicle's huge dimensions. The soldier standing beside the vehicle provides comparison in terms of size.

Right: The development of armored mine-removal vehicles culminated in the 130-ton "Räumer S" created by the Krupp Works of Essen in 1944. It is scarcely believable that a prototype of this vehicle, shown in the drawing at right, was built before the war ended. The four gigantic wheels had a diameter of 2.7 meters. They were meant to provide sufficient ground clearance to protect the vehicle and its crew from exploding mines. After the test model was built, though, it was found that the ground pressure was remarkably high. Thus further work on this device was halted.

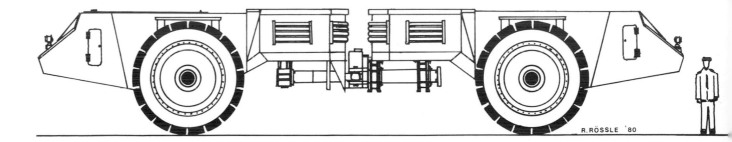

R. RÖSSLE '80

Bridgelayers

In the Polish campaign, the quick Panzer advances proved to be the German Wehrmacht's most powerful weapon. In spite of that, it could not be helped that their advance was slowed because bridges had been blown up. Thus in the same year a solution was sought that would hasten the overcoming of such obstacles. The building of bridgelayers on tank chassis, a means now common to all armies, was already considered at that time. In October 1939 the firms of Krupp and Magirus were given contracts to develop such vehicles on the chassis of the battle tanks. By the beginning of 1940, prototypes from both firms (2 Krupp, 4 Magirus) were finished, differing in the Panzer IV only as to their means of placing the 9-meter bridge. Shortly after they were delivered, they were assigned to the engineers of the 1st Panzer Division for troop testing. In May 1940, the 2nd, 3rd, 5th and 10th Panzer Divisions were also equipped with four bridgelayers each. Although further orders were planned for the future, all contracts were canceled just a month later, in June 1940, so that the monthly production of the Panzer IV tank could be increased. Thus deliveries of the only bridgelayers built in large quantities came to an end. There was also one test vehicle made by Magirus and based on the Panzer IIb and the Krupp bridgelayer, which used running gear with torsion-bar suspension, further developed by the firm's own design bureau for the

This Bridgelayer IV (Krupp version) was halted by damaged tracks during an advance in the west. Tank tracks were already worn out after 800 kilometers at that time. By the war's end, numerous improvements extended their life expectancy to 1500-2000 km for medium tanks. (BA)

Right: Remarkable equipment was built to form bridges quickly. Here a Panzer II crosses a combination of two bridgelayers on the Panzer IA chassis. 7th Panzer Division, autumn 1939.

Panzer IV. A special project was the infantry assault footbridge, also developed by Magirus early in 1940. Unlike the vehicles already described, it did not form a complete bridge, but just a runway for foot soldiers, which consisted of an extending fire ladder. But this assault bridge could also be expanded for the use of motorized units by placing planks between two extended ladders in parallel positions. Since the two finished test models did not completely fulfill the hopes placed in them during action in France and Russia, no others were built.

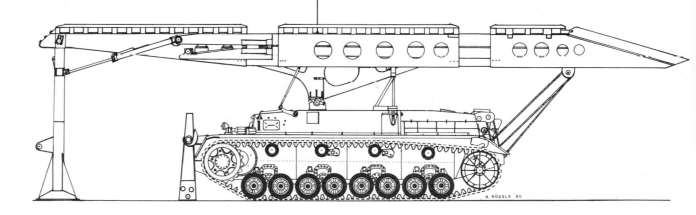

Upper right: In addition to Krupp, Magirus also worked on the construction of a bridgelayer, using the standard chassis of the Panzer IV, Type D. Essentially, the two versions differed in their method of placing the bridge. Apparently the Magirus system was more successful, for of the first twelve vehicles that were delivered, Krupp built only two.

Right: Here the Bridgelayer IV (Magirus) presumably needed only to close the gap between the already existing floating bridge made of wooden plates and the land. The rack on which the portable bridge was carried can be seen especially clearly here. It was carried so that it could be turned, and could be tilted at the desired angle by hydraulic rams. While marching, it was held in place by a network of ropes attached to the rear of the vehicle, and also supported by a transverse rack. (BA)

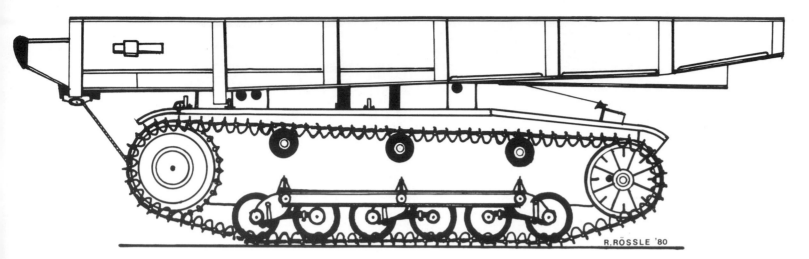

Left: A retired Panzer IIb chassis was also equipped by the Magirus firm with a so-called "fast bridge" for crossing short obstacles in the terrain. Unlike the vehicles already described, it did not unload the bridge by a complex mechanism but simply folded it backward. Only one prototype of this tank was built.

Right: Since not all the armored engineers could be equipped with the few existing bridgelayers, the troops modified available tanks to carry bridges. One was this Panzer II, on which the two pieces of the fast bridge are carried, blocked up on the front of the vehicle and lashed in place. This picture was taken during the French campaign in 1940.

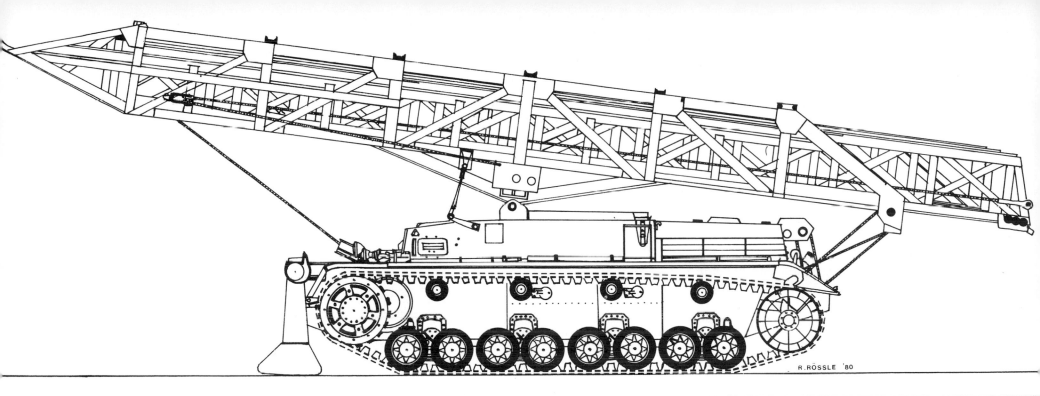

R. RÖSSLE '80

Above: A rarity among the bridgelayers was the so-called "infantry assault footbridge" created by Magirus, which was meant to help foot soldiers cope with obstacles more easily. When two vehicles were used together, a roadway could be made out of planks between the two parallel ladders, allowing motorized units to cross the bridge as well.

Right: After its first, not very successful action in France, the two prototypes of the "infantry assault footbridge" were sent to Russia, where they were lost. The one shown here seems to have driven over a mine, which damaged the running gear considerably. The network of ropes at the rear, with which the ladder was lashed down during marches, can be seen clearly here.

Recovery Tanks

Shortly after the first Tiger I and Panther units were established, it became apparent that the 18-ton towing tractors used until then to tow the Panzer III and IV were not capable of handling these new heavy tanks. Thus it became necessary to develop a new recovery vehicle on a tracked chassis. But since such a chassis was not available, makeshift combinations of vehicles, usually consisting of two or three 18-ton types, had to be used in the meantime.

Attempts were made at first to solve the problem with a two-wheeled recovery device that could be hooked onto any tank chassis. The device included both a cable winch and a ground spur. To use it, the spur was driven firmly into the ground and the damaged tank was pulled by the winch. It was then fastened to the recovery vehicle by a coupling and towed away. It was hoped that the outmoded chassis of the 38 (t) and Panzer III tanks could be used. It soon became obvious, though, that the first measure had completely insufficient pulling power as did the Panzer III, especially with the coupling, which was inclined to break because of its low-lying attachment to the Panzer III chassis. Thus the decision had to be made, for good or ill, to make some of the costly Panther chassis available for rebuilding into recovery vehicles. This "Bergepanther" ("Recovery Panther") had both

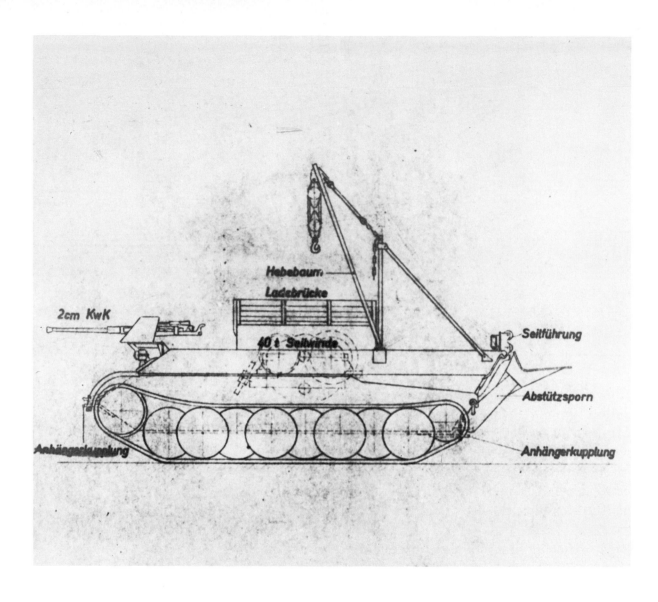

the winch and the ground spur built into or directly attached to the vehicle. The first "Recovery Panthers" reached the front in 1944, after thorough testing at the Kummersdorf testing facility, and proved themselves splendidly. The "Bergetiger" ("Recovery Tiger"), was built in very small numbers and much resembled the "Recovery Panther" in its equipment.

Right: In the Bergepanzer III, tested at the Kummersdorf proving ground as of early 1944, the winch and ground spur were not yet built into or attached to the vehicle, but were towed on a separate two-wheeled trailer. In use, the damaged tank was supposed to be towed out with this "anchor" until it could be coupled to the recovery tank and then towed away. (BA)

Below: Despite their inadequate towing power, 106 of the Bergepanzer 38 (t) were built by the Böhmisch-Mährische Motorenwerke in 1944. Rebuilt "Hetzer" chassis were used for 64 of them. In combat areas, a winch was attached, as it was to the Bergepanther.

Right: Here a damaged Panzer IV is being towed by a Bergepanzer III. It is linked to the towing vehicle by a rod coupling. Because of the low attachment point on the vehicle, this coupling often broke off, as seen in the photo. (BA)

Upper left: A first-type "Bergepanther", also shown in the drawing on page 38, seen here at the Kummersdorf proving ground, where the vehicle was tested thoroughly in 1944. The 2 cm KwK, attached to the first types for short-range self-defense, can be seen with its shield. The auxiliary crane has been dismantled into its component parts, which are attached to the side of the body. (BA)

The pictures at upper right and lower left show details of the spur used on the "Bergepanther." It could be raised and lowered by means of the winch and cable; in use (above) it was rammed firmly into the ground. Thus it was possible to recover even the 70-ton "King Tiger."

Above: For the development of the 40-ton cable winch for the "Bergepanther", an already existing design dating from 1940 was utilized. At that time the MAN firm had designed an eight-wheeled amphibious special engineer vehicle in which a winch of similar capability to the one needed now had been installed for the removal of roadblocks and other obstacles. The cable drum, with the cable wound on it, can be seen at right; behind it are the two drive plates, resting on two shafts. The winch received its power from the vehicle's engine via a shaft and rollers. (BA)

Right: A look into the "crew compartment" of the Bergepanther, which could be covered only by a tarpaulin. In front, on the housing, is the mount for the 2 cm KwK. (BA)

Upper left and above: Front and side views of the later version of the "Bergepanther", with a twin machine gun in place of the 2 cm KwK. The front view shows the mount of the anti-aircraft machine gun at the left and the three steps used by the crew when entering the vehicle. The removable auxiliary crane has been removed; it was used to exchange heavy spare parts. (2xBA)

Left: Here the ground spur has been brought all the way up, as was customary only when marching. The brackets on the side held a wooden plank which could be placed under a vehicle or used to push it in rough country. (BA)

One of the few action photos of the "Bergepanther" shows it with a Panzer V in tow. Both vehicles lack the customary track aprons. The boxy body of the "Bergepanther", in which the 40-ton cable winch was situated, is temporarily covered with roofing material. The weapons have been removed. (BA)

Left: Another picture of the Bergepanther in action, with the 1st Panzer Division in Hungary in 1945.

Above and left: In addition to the Bergetiger on the production chassis, the Porsche firm also built five towing vehicles for the heavy antitank units in 1943, on the basis of the Tiger P. The vehicles were equipped with extra armor plate and had a raised area at the rear which housed the crew. A 7.62 mm MG 34 was provided for close-range self-defense. Unlike all other recovery tanks, the type on the Tiger P chassis had no special equipment (such as a cable winch) for moving disabled tanks except an auxiliary crane and wooden planks.

Right: During the war, a snowplow on the Panzer IV chassis, with a blade three meters across, was also planned. One of the few prototypes to be built underwent thorough testing at the Arlberg Pass in Austria, where this picture was taken. (BA)

Technical Data

Explosive Charge Carriers

Type	B IV Type A	(B)B IV Type C	Type	B IV Type A	(B)B IV Type C	Type	B IV Type A	(B) IV Type C
Manufacturer	Borgward	Borgward	Manufacturer	Borgward	Borgward	Manufacturer	Borgward	Borgward
Years built	1942-43	1943-44	Years built	1942-43	1943-44	Years built	1942-43	1943-44
Crew	1 man or remote control	1 man or remote control	Steering	Cletrac, outside band	Cletrac, outside band	Track width	200 mm	200 mm
Weight	3600 (4000) kg	5000 kg	Ground clearance	?	?	Fuel capacity	130 liters	123 liters
Length	3650 mm	4100 mm	Armor plate	Front 10, sides 5+8, rear 5+8 mm	Front 20, sides 20, rear ? mm	Fuel consumption	Road 58 l/100 km, off-road 100 l/100 km	Road 80 l/100 km, off-road ?
Width	1800 mm	1830 mm						
Height	185 mm	1250 mm						
Engine	in-line 6 cyl. Borgward 6M 2.3 RTBV	in-line 6 cyl. Borgward 6B 3.8	Armament	500 kg explosive	500 kg explosive	Top speed	38 kph	40 kph
			Tracks	Two, 55 links each, front drive, rear guide wheel, 5 road wheels, no return rollers	Two, 77 links each, front drive, rear guide wheel, 5 road wheels, no return rollers	Ground pressure	0.66 kg/sq.cm	?
Cooling	Water	Water				Climbing ability	24 degrees	24 degrees
Horsepower	49 HP	78 HP				Turning circle	11.5 meters	?
Gears	2 forward, 1 reverse	2 forward, 1 reverse				Suspension	Transverse torsion bars	Transverse torsion bars

Technical Data

Goliath

	Electric type	Gasoline type
Manufacturer	Borgward	Zündapp/Zachertz
Years built	1942	1942-44
Crew	Remote control	Remote control
Weight	370 kg	365 kg
Length	1500 mm	1600 mm
Width	850 mm	850 mm
Height	560 mm	600 mm
Powerplant	2 Bosch MM/RQL 2500/24 RL 2 electric	2-cyl. Zündapp 12.5 HP air-cooled
Horsepower	6.8 HP x 2 = 13.6 HP	12.5 HP
Gears	Two levels	Two forward
Steering	Electromagnetic	Electromagnetic
Ground clearance	114 mm	168 mm
Armor plate	Front 5 mm, other ?	Front 10 mm, other ?
Armament	60 kg explosive	75 or 100 kg explosive
Tracks	Two, 48 links each, front drive, rear guide wheel, 5 road wheels, 3 return rollers	Two, 48 links each, front drive, rear guide wheel, 5 road wheels, 2 return rollers
Track width	160 mm	160 mm
Fuel capacity	–	?
Fuel consumption	–	6 liters/100 km
Top speed	10 kph	11 kph
Ground pressure	?	?
Climbing ability	?	70 degrees
Turning circle	3-4 meters	3-4 meters
Suspension	Coil springs	Coil springs

Springer

Manufacturer	NSU
Years built	1944-45
Crew	1 man or remote control
Weight	2400 kg
Length	3150 mm
Width	1430 mm
Height	1450 mm
Powerplant	4-cyl. in-line Opel 1.5 liter
Cooling	Water
Horsepower	37 HP
Gears	6 forward, 2 reverse
Steering	Mechanical, inside
Ground clearance	230 mm
Armor plate	Front 10, sides 5 mm, rear ?
Armament	300 kg explosive charge
Tracks	Two, 100 links each, front drive, rear guide wheel, 6 overlapping road wheels, no return rollers
Track width	170 mm
Fuel capacity	65 liters
Fuel consumption	22 liters/100 km
Top speed	42 kph
Ground pressure	?
Climbing ability	?
Turning circle	4.0 meters
Suspension	Transverse torsion bars

Above: An engineer, using the controls hanging before him, pilots a Goliath between two armored vehicles.

Opposite page: In the upper photo, the "Goliath" is shown to Hitler.

In the lower photo, the Goliath has just been unloaded from its transport cart and is being prepared for action.

Technical Data

Ammunition Carriers

Type	Pz. IA	Pz. B1
Manufacturer	Daimler-Benz	Borgward
Years built	1934-35	1939-40
Crew	2 men	1 man or remote control
Weight	5000 kg	?
Length	4020 mm	?
Width	2060 mm	?
Height	1400 mm	?
Engine	Krupp M 305 4-cylinder horizontally opposed	Borgward 4M 1, 5P II in-line 4-cyl
Cooling	Air	Water
Horsepower	57 HP	29 HP
Gears	5 forward, 1 reverse	2 forward, 1 reverse
Steering	Krupp clutch-type	Electromagnetic
Ground clearance	295 mm	?
Armor plate	Front 15, 13 mm, sides rear	? ?
Armament	None	None
Tracks	Two, front drive, rear guide wheel, 4 roadwheels, 3 return rollers	Two, front drive, rear guide wheel, 3 road wheels, no return rollers
Track width	280 mm	?
Fuel capacity	144 liters	?
Fuel consumption	100 liters/100 km	15-25 liters/100 km
Top speed	37 kph	2 kph
Ground pressure	0.35 kg/sq. cm	?
Climbing ability	30 degrees	?
Turning circle	?	?
Suspension	Coil & quarter leaf	Torsion bars

Type	VK 301	VK 501
Manufacturer	Borgward	Weserhütte
Years built	1940-42	1943-44
Crew	2 men	5 men
Weight	3500 kg	6000 kg
Length	3570 mm	3830 mm
Width	1830 mm	2220 mm
Height	?	1690 mm
Engine	Borgward 6M 2.3 RTBV 6 cylinders in line	Maybach NL 38 TR 6 cylinders in line
Cooling	Water	Water
Horsepower	49 HP	100 HP
Gears	2 forward, 1 reverse	?
Steering	?	?
Ground clearance	?	?
Armor plate	Front 14.5, sides and rear 10 mm	Front, sides and rear 20 mm
Armament	None	1 machine gun
Tracks	2, front drive, rear guide, 4 road wheels, no return rollers	2, front drive, rear guide, 5 overlapping road wheels, no return rollers
Track width	200 mm	?
Fuel capacity	123 liters	220 liters
Fuel consumption	Road 58 liters /100 km, off-road 100 liters /100 km	100 liters /100 km
Top speed	30 kph	30 kph
Ground pressure	0.66 kg/sq. cm	?
Climbing ability	24 degrees	?
Turning circle	11.5 meters	?
Suspension	?	?